What Do I Do Now, Mom?

Jean D. Crowther

What Do I Do Now, Mom?

Jean D. Crowther

Revised Edition: July, 1993

International Standard Book Number
0-88290-134-6

Library of Congress Catalog Card Number
80-82257

Horizon Publishers' Catalog and Order Number
2014

Fifth Printing, July 1993

Printed and distributed
in the United States of America by

Horizon
Publishers
& Distributors, Incorporated
50 South 500 West • P.O. Box 490
Bountiful, Utah 84011-0490

To my daughters

Lisa,

Sharon, and

Bethany

who have become

beautiful

women.

Contents

But Mom . . .

I remember coming home from school many years ago in "almost tears" because my 7th grade class had spent the afternoon learning how to dance. In those days, dancing meant holding onto each other in a particular position and the girl tried to follow the boy as he moved his feet in a pattern. I had already grown to my adult height and was the tallest person in my class. The 7th grade that year was full of short little boys whose heads didn't even come up to my shoulders. All afternoon they had teased me about my height and my big clumsy feet.

My wise and understanding mother attempted to soothe my frustrations by telling me that girls grew faster than boys and that one of these days the boys would all grow up too. (This proved to be true. Before we were out of high school, they had all passed me in height and were having their own problems with being tall and awkward.) My brokenhearted wail of that afternoon, however, was "But Mom, what do I do *NOW* while I am waiting?"

This is the challenge of our early teenage years. Young girls are impatient. They don't want to wait until life catches up to them. They are anxious to do something to solve their problems and to answer their questions *now*.

So to all of those girls (and their families) who are wondering what they can do while they are waiting to become a beautiful young woman, here are some suggestions about the areas that seem most troublesome for young teenagers. I have divided these suggestions into six chapters:

- ★ Improving your appearance
- ★ Refining your personality
- ★ Enjoying your family
- ★ Making good friends
- ★ Developing fun relationships with boys
- ★ Gaining a lasting testimony of God

Each chapter will cover things that you can change *now*—problem areas where your efforts can really influence your growth and help you become the kind of woman you want to be.

There are problems you can solve, and abilities that you can develop right *now*, while you are waiting for the rest of your life to happen! This book will help you do it!

It has been said that:

There are two ways to get to the top of an oak tree.
You can climb up it—or you can sit on an acorn.

So get off of your acorn and start climbing!

Seven Magic Keys For Looking Your Best

"I look like a mess!!!"

Oh, oh! You overslept and you're running late. It's time to leave for school and you just aren't ready yet. Your hair refuses to cooperate. You can't find your favorite pair of pants (you will next Saturday when you clean out underneath your bed), and you just can't decide what to wear. Nothing looks right together. You leave several discarded outfits lying around your room as you hurry. To top it all off, a flying glance at the mirror on your way out the door makes you sure that four of those sore spots on your face will be pimples by noon!

Knowing that you don't look your best, you run into the building, only to find yourself greeted by the cutest girl in the school. Well—greeted isn't quite the word—she sort of half-smiles as you dash past. As you race to beat the tardy bell, you begin to wonder if she was smiling hello or thinking that you really looked funny! You just barely slide into your seat for your first class on time, but can't even listen to the teacher. All you can think about are your mismatched clothes and your uncurled hair. You spend the complete period tearing yourself apart, making a list of everything wrong with your appearance. "My hair is a mess. Why couldn't I have been born with naturally-curly hair?" "I have no cute clothes to wear! Anyway, I wouldn't know how to wear them if I did!" "Why do I have such big feet?" "Why am I so awkward and clumsy?" "Why can't I be cute, with a tiny waist?"

As the ruined day goes on, you become more and more sure that all of your problems boil down to one thing:

"I'm so different! *I look horrible!*"

So what can you do about your appearance *now*?

No One Looks Alike

The first thing to do is to realize that every person born on the earth looks different than anyone else. The genes that decide your physical appearance, and those of every human being, have the mathematical possibility for unlimited combinations of physical characteristics. You will never look exactly like someone else (unless you're one of those very rare individuals—an identical twin).

Your physical characteristics do link you together with your family, though. Newborn babies often carry such distinctive features that people say, "She has long fingers just like her grandpa's," "Her head is shaped like Bob's," or "Look at her long curly eyelashes, they're just like yours!" You do look like other members of your family. Perhaps you do have a nose that's a fraction larger than the average. You probably have at least one parent with a bigger one. (Remember the song from *Saturday's Warrior*? "We all have Daddy's nose.")"My goodness, look at Uncle John! His nose is huge and often seems to be glowing red—especially when he has a cold! You still all love each other.

The physical characteristics you were born with will be with you always. Some of them are much, much better than "average." But others aren't quite as good. You can modify some of them, but many are unchangable. They just aren't your "best" features. It won't do any good to let yourself worry about the less-attractive parts of your physical appearance ruin your life. You are that way because it is part of your individuality. You need to accept what you cannot change.

Most people with serious physical disabilities learn to overcome the need for pity and the temptation to mope around wishing that things were different. You can do the same thing with your minor imperfections. If your eyes are bad enough to need glasses, wear them (or convince your parents to investigate contact lenses). If you have inherited taller or larger bones than you would like, or are ten inches shorter than others your age, moaning won't help. No one yet has been able to change their height one way or another by complaining. A wise man once said,

> **Nature does not demand that we be perfect,**
> **It only requires that we grow.**

There are many things about your appearance, though, that you can do something about. Here are Seven Magic Keys. They really will work a magical change in your appearance if you carefully follow them in order. Apply them wisely and faithfully and they truly will help you improve the way you look, *now*!

Key #1—Stand Up Tall and Scrub

Susan's mother sighed as she watched her tall, slender daughter walk into the room after school. She bit her tongue as she said to herself . . .

"I will not mention her posture one more time today. I've nagged her for three years about standing up straight. I just can't keep on fussing at her!"

Suddenly she was amazed as she watched Susan walk over to the large mirror and straighten up her shoulders into good posture. Susan relaxed back into her normal slouch and then straightened up again.

Her mother held her breath as Susan said, "Guess what happened to me today? Brent Johnson spoke to me! He actually stopped in the hall and said, 'Hi!' Oh, Mom, he is so much taller than I am! I had to look up to see him! He said, 'Hey, it's nice to look into a face when I talk. All I ever see are the tops of heads!' Maybe it's not so bad to be tall!!"

Susan had learned a very important principle that day: "Being tall has some real advantages." She also realized that she actually looked lots better when she stood up straight.

Everyone looks better with good posture. It can make a tall girl look better, even glamorous. Good posture will also add to your height if you are on the shorter end of the scale. And it will take inches off your waist and other problem areas.

You don't have to take my word for it. Stand in front of a mirror with your normal stance. Then straighten up into good posture. You can't make excuses to a mirror!

Humped-forward shoulders will cause your back to fall out of its proper line. Your tummy will poke out, your midriff will relax and your bustline will sag. A relaxed slouch will even cause your hips to bulge forward and look larger. The muscles that should support you properly will eventually loose their tone and you can spend a lifetime looking lumpy!

Imagine a rope coming out of the top of your head. It's attached to a pulley on the ceiling. As you stand in front of the mirror, someone behind you begins to pull that rope tighter. The top of your head is pulled up. Your shoulders are lifted up and back (try to make your shoulder blades meet in back). Your bust becomes higher (and appears larger and prettier), and your upper body falls into its natural place. This causes the muscles around your waist, tummy, and hips to tighten so you appear slimmer.

Now, don't you look better? All of your clothes will look better, too, when they are hanging from the right places instead of being forced over bumps caused by poor posture.

If your mirror test convinced you that you can work on your posture, here are three easy two-minute exercises to do each day to help your body relearn correct posture:

1. Standing in front of a mirror (if available—if not, your imagination will have to help here), think of the pulley and rope lifting and straightening your body. As your body reaches its correct posture, hold it there for ten very slow counts. Relax and then repeat the pulley tightening five times. Remember to not become rigid as you lift your body. Good posture is relaxed—not a stiff "military attention" pose.

2. Each day, stand against a wall as if you were being measured for your height. Pull your body into line against the wall. Try to force your back to touch the wall at your waistline. (You may not be able to touch the wall there, but trying to do so will flatten your tummy anyway.) Memorize what your body feels like in this position. Ten times a day, stop what you are doing for a few seconds and pull your body into that position without the wall to help you. (Go back to a wall when you need help remembering.) As it becomes more natural, you will find yourself in this position more often.

3. The old-fashioned way of balancing a book on top of your head is a great exercise! Two minutes a day walking with a book will train your body to remember good posture as you move.

Congratulations! After a month of faithful exercises, your posture will be visibly improved and you will have established habits that will last for a lifetime if you'll keep reinforcing them. But what about the scrub part of the first magic key?

Why scrub?? Teenage years are times of hormonal changes and your bodily secretions go haywire. Anti-perspirants are suddenly needed, your hair is oily all the time, and pimples and blackheads break out all over. It becomes necessary to wash off the extra oils that cause the problem.

Generally, for most girls, if you wash your face *at least* four times a day most of the skin problems will be solved. That's true, because pimples and blackheads are simply skin pores clogged with dirt and oil. If you keep the dirt and oil off of your skin, they will have less chance to develop. This is especially true as you begin to use make-up. As Confucious could have said:

Washee face four times a day,
Makee pimples go away.

Besides, each time you wash your face, you get the added health benefit of washing your hands. This will reduce the number of germs on your hands and will probably greatly lessen your chance of getting sick. Your family will also benefit when you don't bring home every virus and infection going around at school.

Hair is easier to style when it's newly washed, too. A brightly-scrubbed face and shining, clean hair might not be the high-fashion look of the day, but it is surely an acceptable substitute in most situations. If you know that you are as neat and clean as you can be, you can stand up proudly in most situations without feeling like an "ugly duckling."

So the first magic key for improving your appearance is *stand up tall and scrub.*

Key #2—Decide What You Can Change

Take another good look at your friend—the mirror. What can you change now that will improve your appearance the most? Is it the way you style your hair? your clothes? your make-up techniques? your weight? Identify in your mind the one thing that, if it were changed, would make the biggest difference. Be very honest with yourself, but make sure that it is something that can be changed. You would do well to have someone help you in this decision (try your mother, or another interested adult).

You probably are thinking, "I have too many things to change to choose just one!" But remember,

> **Anyone can eat an elephant if you cut it up into small enough pieces.**

What if I asked you to stand over on the other side of the room to catch twelve tennis balls as I threw them to you; and then I threw the whole box at you at once! How many could you catch? You would probably be caught on the nose by one ball and would be quite lucky to catch even one of the others. But if I threw the balls to you one at a time, you would probably catch every one of them.

Just like the tennis balls, it is usually almost impossible to work on several problems at one time (unless they are very closely-related, like keeping your hair clean and learning to style it better). If you limit yourself to one problem at a time, you will be more successful. You can get around to the others later.

Choose your problem and then write it down. Write exactly what you want to change and write it in a positive way:

"I will develop better taste in clothes."
"I will learn to style my hair."
"I will loose ten pounds."
"I will stop biting my nails."

Then write another sentence on how you could complete the goal:

"I will study my figure and fashions and find out what looks good on me."
"I will save my money, have my hair cut, and ask them to teach me how to style it."
"I will go on a diet starting tomorrow at breakfast."
"I will keep my hands out of my mouth."

Writing down the goal and trying to decide how to accomplish it is the first step towards change. A wise man once observed,

A goal that is not written down is only a wish,
and wishes don't come true.

Key #3—Seek Help

As you write down the goal, write the name of someone who can help you. Choose someone you think knows how to do what you are trying to learn. This could be your mother, your sister, an aunt, your advisor, or even a friend your own age. All she needs is to know how to do what you are trying to learn, better than you do. Go to her and ask, "How can I learn . . .? Will you show me how?"

Most people are willing to help. Occasionally you might catch someone at a busy time and not get a good response. That doesn't mean she can't or won't help. Try her again, or seek out someone else. But keep trying until you find your own "expert" to help you learn your needed skill.

Key #4—Practice

It will take effort to change years of habit or to learn a new skill. The more you have to change, the more effort will be required. There might even be times that you become discouraged and are ready to quit the whole idea. But that is a stage in your learning, too. You need to remember,

> **Don't confuse the things you *won't* do,
> with the things you *can't* do."**

Be patient with yourself. You'll probably have times that you goof up your project pretty badly.

So don't try something brand new just before a big event in your life. Be sure to practice make-up techniques at times that you can wash your face off and change back to the "old-standby" look if you fail. The "wicked-witch-of-the-west" makeup will cause a sensation at a Halloween party but probably won't be too appropriate for a stake Mia Maid Standards Night.

Be sure to let your parents know of your plans. They can lend valuable support to your efforts, and you might prevent a crisis like the one that my friend Cathy experienced.

Cathy was trying to change her appearance by applying these same principles that I am teaching you. She decided that the one thing she needed to change the most was her hair style that she thought made her look like a little girl. She talked some ideas over with a friend or two and then decided to find out what a beautician had to offer.

There Cathy made her big mistake. She felt that her mother wouldn't like her to have her waist-long hair cut, so Cathy didn't ask her. She quietly took her own baby-sitting money and went to the appointment.

The inexperienced beautician had just learned the latest cut and talked Cathy into trying it because "It's the latest style and looks cute on anyone!"

Her mother literally "fell apart at the seams" when Cathy arrived home. It took many days for the crisis to simmer down enough that they could even talk to one another. There were several very stormy and tearful sessions, with Cathy defending her right to have it cut because "it's my own hair" and "everyone wears their hair this way now." But then Cathy began to realize that she had made a mistake. This latest style really didn't look good on her and she regretted her hasty decision. She began to let her hair grow out immediately and is now wearing a slightly shortened version of her original hair style because it makes her look her best.

So talk about the project with your parents before you get very far into it. A decision that will rather permanently alter your appearance (or cost money) really needs permission from your parents, even if you have the money to finance it yourself.

Key #5—Be Yourself

Remember that you are a distinct individual, a special "one-of-a-kind" girl. It isn't necessary for you to look exactly like your friend or idol to be in style. You won't—even if you try! Sometimes what looks good on someone else will look perfectly terrible on you. The current styles can, and should, be adapted by you, choosing what part of them will help you look your very best. Don't try to be a carbon copy of someone else. Develop your own style out of what is popular now.

You have an inborn sense of what is modest. But remember, the fashion world has rejected such modesty. Clothing designers make their living by developing extreme fashions so that you have to buy all new things to keep in style. Evaluate the latest styles and adopt what is new and different only if it can be worn in a modest manner *and* if it is becoming on you.

And don't try to look too grown-up too soon. You will have many years to look mature. If you are now 12, find out what makes you look cute as a 12-year old and don't try to copy the high school styles too closely. You'll look funny and out of place if you do. Take your time! You'll have a whole year to look 17 when the time comes. Be patient with what you are *now* and develop your own look for your current age.

Key #6—Don't Keep Your Goal A Secret

You have already talked your idea over with your parents, of course, but if your project is one where others can help you too, let them know about it. How many diets have failed because someone unknowingly tempted the dieter with an irresistible goodie?

If weight control is your goal, let your whole family know, especially those who cook. Keep them advised of your progress (or lack of it). And let a few special friends in on the secret, too. They can all help decide interesting things to do that won't require eating. Perhaps some of them will join you at the salad bar, too. A cheering section can do wonders for your morale.

Make sure that dieting is what you really need. You might think that you are overweight (it is a natural tendency for a girl your age to worry about being too fat), when perhaps a good exercise program to tighten up your TV muscles is what is really needed. There are many good articles in current magazines or inexpensive books that will help you with this goal. It is easy to become an expert on this subject. Get some friends or family members to join you here, too. Jogging is much more fun when done in a group!

I made this
special dessert
just for you.

While we're on the subject of food, remember that a good balanced diet is very important for you now. It aids your proper growth now. But what you eat in your teenage-developing years will also affect your health for your entire lifetime. Studies have shown that when girls eat poorly as teenagers, devouring lots of junk-type foods and not enough nutritious meals, there is a very high chance that their babies and children will have serious health problems. So your mother's reminders to drink your milk and eat your vegetables is probably helping her grandchildren have more healthy bodies!

You have a better chance to achieve any goal you set if you have a team supporting you. Very few people would enjoy playing basketball if there wasn't someone else to play with them. Enlist a team of your own to help you in your "new-you" project. It will be easier and more fun to accomplish.

Key #7—Act "As If"

This seventh magic key is the best one, and often the easiest, to use. It has been called a theory, but it really works! It has helped many thousands of people achieve what they dreamed of and will work for you, too. It is:

> **If you want something to be different than it is right now, act "as if" it has already happened and it will become yours.**

Remember when you were little and used to play pretend? "Let's play like we are beautiful princesses," or "Play like I'm the mother and you're the baby." Didn't those times seem real to you?

You were playing with the "as if" principle. You acted as if you were princesses and so you felt like you were princesses. You are now going to play the same game a little more seriously. You'll end up turning into what you pretend.

You want to become more beautiful. As you walk past a mirror, say to yourself, "I'll play like this dress looks pretty on me." Without even thinking about it, your shoulders will

straighten into better posture and your self-confidence will grow. The dress really will look better because you are acting "as if" it is beautiful and others will see it that way.

I remember one evening when I spilled milk all over the front of a light pants outfit. I was on my way to a very important meeting and was running a little late (the reason for the spilled milk—I tried to eat a bite of supper in the car). There was no time to try to repair the damage (milk leaves dark spots when it dries on light material), so I had no other choice than to walk into that meeting with spots all over my clothes. I acted "as if" there was nothing the matter with my clothes and before long I had almost forgotten the problem. I doubt that anyone there remembers me as the "lady with the milk spots" either. Some people might call this "bluffing" or "faking," but it is a valid principle, and it can be used for growth.

As you pretend to be something, your desire to learn to be what you are pretending will increase. Your interests in that area will develop and you will want to know more about it. It is an ever-rising spiral.

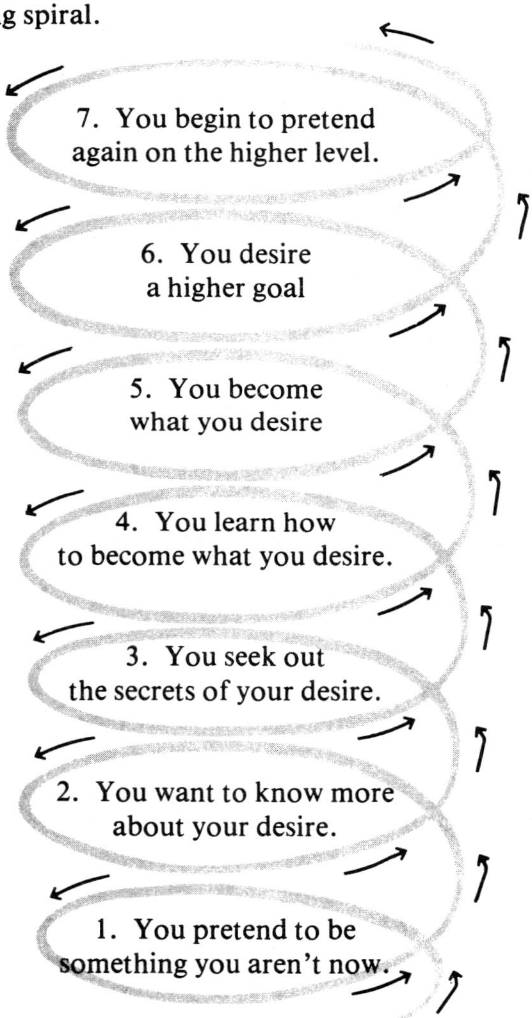

The "As If" Principle At Work

Even in the beginning stages of pretending, if you go into any situation acting as if you know what you are doing, you probably will do well. Others will believe in you and then you will begin to believe in yourself. This is good! It is not hypocrisy! It is a real tool for helping yourself reach higher than you are now.

Acting "as if" will work in most areas of your life. But it especially is an interesting way to help you change your appearance. Your mind is the control center of your body and you can look like what you think you want to look like.

Try It!

And finally, there is truth in Mother's soothing words,

"Don't worry, dear. Someday you will become beautiful."

"The boys will all grow up and become taller than you are."

"Your face will clear up."

"Your body will even itself out so you won't be so clumsy."

Time is on your side! If you can be patient, it will help you become the girl of your dreams.

But if you follow the Seven Magic Keys, you can do something about some of your worries right *now*. Get busy and have fun learning to improve your appearance and becoming a better "you."

Polishing Off Your Personality Problems

You Can Be Anything You Really Want To Be

Personality is the part of you that makes you act the way you do (whether your actions are good or bad), and determines how you feel about what you do. Your personality is developing right now into what you'll be as an adult. A noted social researcher recently stated that,

> **Adolescence is a time of rebirth. It is the time to find out "who I am."**

The discovery of yourself as a real person is exciting. You are not just your mother's little girl, or your Dad's good buddy. You are *you*—a real person, a worthwhile individual with adult ideas developing.

In the midst of this exciting discovery though, remember that these growing-up years are a major part of life, too. You are living right now, not just preparing for life. So often a young girl "can hardly wait until . . ." and she forgets to live life right now.

I was taught that "you can be anything you really want to be!"

Do you desire to be gracious and lovely?
Do you want to be able to talk with anyone about anything?
Do you want to have a sense of humor and entertain everyone with your clever comments?
Do you want to be well-educated?
Do you want to get ahead financially?
Do you want to have fun in any situation?
Do you want to become a loving and capable mother of a large family?
Do you want to be chosen as a beloved wife?

All of these seeds, and more, are within you right now. And any of the above descriptions could fit each of you in the years to come. You begin to become them right now. If you don't make an effort to develop into the person you want to be, you might develop into the kind of person you don't want to be—or even into not much of anyone at all.

"As If" Works in Developing Your Personality

Probably the best place to put the "as if" principle to work is in developing your personality. Let me tell you a true story.

I first met Jennie when she was a timid, shy thirteen-year-old girl. She didn't have any friends. She spent most of her time trying to quietly stay away from people. In fact, she often would seem to disappear into the background when she was in a group. No one really knew that she was even there.

Then Jennie was taught about the "as if" principle and was challenged to try it out. She was overwhelmed with the idea.

"I can't," she wailed.

But Jennie was very unhappy with her life and really longed for friends, so she finally agreed to try.

There were three other girls in her class at church, but she had never responded to their friendship offers so they had begun to ignore her. Jennie was counselled to begin with them. She was to act "as if" they were already her friends, and to say "hi" to them each time she saw them. She was not only to say "hi" but was also to make at least one other comment—even if she could only think of something like "It sure is cold, isn't it?"

This was very hard for Jennie to force herself to do. It was so different from her usual way of walking around school looking at the ground that she became very frustrated.

"It's just an act," she cried, "Everyone can see right through me. They think I'm strange!"

She spent several nights in tears because she was so sure that the three girls were making fun of her. But that wasn't true.

The girls in her class were quite amazed at her efforts to begin a conversation and they began to accept her painful attempts. They even began to speak to her first. Jennie soon found that it wasn't at all hard to talk with them. Her self-confidence was bolstered as her friendship with the three church girls began to blossom. As they included her in their circle at school, she began to feel more confident about speaking to others. It took many months but her circle of friends began to grow.

Jennie has always had a natural gift for finding the clever side of a happening and had entertained her family with her funny way of telling a story. As she began to be friendly, she began to share this gift with others. People began to enjoy talking with her. She slowly changed into a more open and friendly person as her desire to be around others grew. Even the boys began to enjoy her company and the upward spiral of her personality change began.

By the time she graduated from high school (just five years after she put the "as if" principle to work) she was a member of a large group of boys and girls who were the leaders at school and church. The once shy and timid thirteen-year-old wallflower had turned into a self-confident young lady who was able to go forward into life unafraid. It was a complete reversal of personality.

You probably aren't in the same situation as Jennie. Your self-esteem and knowledge of your own ability are probably much higher than hers was. But everyone can improve, and you can change into a better person than you are now by acting "as if." And if you are a young girl who is afraid of people as Jennie was, believe in her story and try her solution. It is true! It really happened!! You can do it, too!!!

Nobody Likes Me!

There will be times that each of you might not feel accepted by your friends. This is a very normal situation. I know that it doesn't help your hurt feelings to say that you are normal—but it is right. During teenage years, your friendships may change several times, because everyone is growing in different ways. Sometimes you will be left out of a group, or be very lonesome. You might even have your feelings badly hurt.

But even the most confident-looking people have the same types of problems. They have just learned to be more skillful at hiding their feelings. The "I'm tough!" attitude is often necessary to cover up sore and bleeding feelings that have been hurt. It might not make you accepted by those who hurt you, but it will help you live with your unhappiness better.

Your friends play a very important part in your personality development. Your need for their acceptance is probably the greatest force in your life right now. You probably want to be *just like them.*

You may even feel that to be different, or to dress differently, or to be expected to act differently is some kind of a crime. Certainly it is a social goof to be "different." In most ways, doing what the group does is good and right!!

Your friends give you a sense of identity. You get your ideas of what is acceptable and what is right and wrong from them. You have someone your own age to measure yourself against. They feel the same way about life as you do now. And friends provide a built-in group to go places with.

But you must be careful. Choose friends with caution and watch where they are heading. Be sure that their destination is where you want to go. You will become like your friends—

are they what you want to become? Remember, the eternal things of life are not worth trading away for popularity. As President Kimball counseled the young women of the Church,

> **In the midst of the here and now,**
> **don't forget to live for the there and then.**

Choose wisely, and live for eternity, not just for today.

Why Do I Feel So Good And Then So Bad?

The air was so biting cold that it made Laurie's cheeks sting, but she felt great! It had been a good day at school and everything had gone well. She had the whole afternoon ahead of her and not too much to do. As she walked quickly up the hill, she began to plan her afternoon.

"I'll get something to eat and then relax for a while. I've earned a break. That one page of math won't take too long—maybe I'll even have time to polish my nails."

No one was in the house as she entered.

"That's funny" she thought. "Wonder where Mom is?"

Laurie raided the refrigerator, leaving a mess in the kitchen, and then plopped down in front of the TV for cartoons. An hour later the phone rang.

"Laurie, I've been held up at the Dentist. How is the meatloaf coming?" her mother asked.

"What meatloaf?" Laurie cried.

"Oh, Laurie!" her mother wailed, "I left you a note right out on the counter. I wanted you to get the meatloaf and potatoes out of the fridge and into the oven. Now supper won't be ready for your father before his early meeting. I wish you could be a little more responsible!"

As her mother was talking, Laurie found the note under the bottle of milk she had left on the counter. Her mother, after asking why she was watching television before homework was done, told her what to do to salvage some supper plans and hung up.

"I don't know why she's so mad," mumbled Laurie. "I really didn't see the dumb note!"

As Laurie followed mother's instructions, the phone rang again. It was her friend, Ann.

"Have you gotten to the third page of our math homework yet? It's hard!!" Ann asked.

"Third page!" shouted Laurie. "I thought we only had one page."

"No, you weren't listening," answered Ann. "Mr. Dennis said that the first page was really easy so we should go on to the next two pages. And they are really hard! I've been working on the first 3 problems almost ever since I got home. You're in real trouble if you haven't started yet."

Laurie hung up the phone with a slam.

"Where had her beautiful day gone? Her mother was mad, her dad would be upset about supper, and that Mr. Dennis! He must think that all they had to do was his math! Why did people have to ruin her day?"

Laurie was responding to her problems with some of the mood changes that teenagers have. The hormones that change your physical body cause the same kind of changes in your feelings. You change from happy to sad very suddenly, often even without the frustrations Laurie had.

You can compare your mood changes to a pendulum on a very long wire. When you were in grade school, it hung pretty steady, moving when acted upon from the outside, but usually moving with very little swing.

But in your early teenage years, the pendulum begins to swing. Sometimes it has a very wide swing and you feel abrupt mood changes. Your beautiful day can come crashing around you in an instant, or your moods can be lightened by the sight of an opening blossom. You change so fast that you often don't know what to do with yourself or even what to expect. This can be very frustrating to yourself and others around you. Other days your mood pendulum has a more controlled swing, but still your moods change.

As your hormone changes settle down during your later teenage years and you gain more maturity, your mood pendulum's swing will moderate. But all your life, as a female, you will be influenced in your moods as your hormonal balances and bodily rhythms ebb and flow in their established cycles. You will learn to handle these changes better than you do right now, but you will still have them.

I Get So Frustrated!

Some days you might wake up feeling grumpy and even socially unacceptable. But you'll have to live out that day anyway. The kindest thing that you can do is to control yourself around others so that you don't ruin their days, too. It will take a little effort, but your family and friends will be thankful for your efforts and will treat you more kindly because you tried. You will learn the truth in the old saying,

> **Smile and the world smiles with you,**
> **weep and you weep alone.**

But this doesn't always work, and you might continue to feel badly. You can't really put a finger on what is the matter—you're just "out-of-sorts." When you feel this way, you possibly will unconciously seek out an argument. It seems that when you are unhappy with yourself, you try to find some other reason to be mad, often going out to scout up an argument. When you find one, you don't have to be mad at yourself anymore; you can be angry at another person.

If you find your argument when you are in the bad mood I have described, it is likely to be a very bitter one. Words spoken during such occasions are difficult to overcome. Put a red flag out in your mind when you feel frustrated. You could really hurt someone you love without meaning to.

Here are five better things to try when you feel "out-of-sorts":

1. *Do something for someone else*—even if it is a tiny thing like secretly making your sister's bed, or unloading the dishwasher when it's not your job; it will help. The larger the task you accomplish, the greater you will feel. You will get your mind off your own self and this will cause your troubles to fade. A Russian poet said,

That which you give away is yours,
—that which you keep is lost.

2. *Start every day with prayer and scripture reading*—even when you don't feel like it. Your prayer should ask for help in feeling better.

   And all things whatsoever ye shall ask in prayer, believing, ye shall receive. (Matt. 21:22)

   Your mood is almost sure to soften as you plead with the Lord to help you change in your attitude.

3. *Wear something that you know makes you look your best.* My mother, who sewed most of the clothes for her six daughters, sometimes made what she called a "jackpot dress." These dresses, because of their pattern, type of material, style or color, fit the wearer beautifully and made her look "perfect." You will find that you have a few of the same "jackpot" clothes, too. Wear them when you wake up with the "icky-blahs," and you might feel better just because you look better.

4. Put aside a little money for those moody days and plan to *buy a small treat for yourself* later in the day. Your spirits will lift all day as you look forward to the unaccustomed goodie. Think about all the different things you could buy with the money. Anticipation is the spirit-lifter in this plan.

5. *Do something physical.* Make your body work and soon you will feel better, too. My childhood home was very close to one of the LDS temples. I enjoyed walking over to the beautiful gardens that surrounded it. The sweet spirit that existed there would calm my troubled mind so much that sometimes my mother would suggest that it was time for me to "go walk around the temple." The physical benefits of a brisk walk or jog or some type of sports activity will serve this same purpose for you.

I Don't Know What I Want To Be!

That's the whole exciting part of your life right now! You *don't* have to know for sure what you want to be yet. This is the time to try things out. Society accepts teenage years as ones where you change and experiment and "do crazy things." You can act silly in a public place (within reason, of course), try out a new hairstyle (with parent's permission), wear new and unusual clothing (if your budget will allow them) or even change the style of your handwriting.

You are searching for the "real you"! Choose an idea or ideal and follow it for a time. Then keep the part of the idea that feels right for you and move on to another, better idea. Reach higher each time—higher than you think you can. Let your natural inclination for wanting things to be perfect lead you to better ideals each time.

Be careful! When I tell you that it's right to experiment with new ideas *I do not* mean that you should try tobacco, alcohol, or drugs! Only unhappiness can come from them. The changes that they make in your life are external ones and you have to keep on using them to re-create the sensations they bring. They turn your eternal spirit away from your seeking for the right kinds of happiness, and draw you into the friends that are not trying for the same goals as you are working towards.

Probably the reason that those drugs are so eternally evil has little to do with the debated facts of their addictive powers. In order to produce the sensations they cause, they all affect some part of the mind. Since the mind is so closely related to your spirit (that part of you that existed long before this life began and will be *you* throughout eternity), you are gambling with very high stakes. What a price you pay throughout the eternities for seeking certain thrills or acceptance from friends here on earth!

"Remember who you are" and who you might become, and don't let anything entice you into participating in experiments with tobacco, alcohol, or drugs. The price you'll have to pay is far too high!

Your friends are going through the same type of personality changes that you are experiencing. They will cause frustrations in your life because of their own problems. It is good practice for you to learn patience with their troubles. Your family goes through it all the time with you!

A flower in the bud stages is lovely, but it lacks the fragrance and color it will eventually have. A bud holds just a promise of beauty. As the blossom opens out into its full glory, all the colors and sweet fragrance are displayed. The promise of beauty is fulfilled.

This is your personality. It is like a handful of soft clay right now. You can, through your own effort, make *you* into the person you want to become.

You can be anything you really want to be—if you want it enough!!

Learning To Love Your Family

"Sue volunteered to stay with the kids while we go out tonight."

Your family is yours. You belong to them. They are a permanent part of you—forever, we hope! You can't change them for another group of people if you are unhappy with them.

Usually you can't even change their attitudes much. Your parents have lived at least twice as long as you have now and they have become pretty set in their ways.

But you can change *your* attitude towards *them* if you need to. Remember that in your pre-mortal life (when you understood all about earth life and what it would be like), you probably made a covenant with these very people that you would be an earthly family together. You knew what kind of parents they would be because you had lived with them and worked together with them there. And because you knew and loved them, you were willing to place yourself under their care and direction here on earth. Remember that the next time you are angry about a rule that your dad makes, or are cross about a task that your mother insists that you complete.

I Have To Do It Their Way

A wise man once asked,

How strict should parents be?
Like the supporting ropes on a young tree.
Every once in a while you loosen up on the rope.
Then one day you find out that it can stand up by itself.

Your family is your security, just like a warm blanket on a cold night. Their love can warm you and heal your bruised ego and torn dreams, and you can count on them to be there when you need them.

Even the house you live in can reflect this love. The next time you approach your home on a dark, stormy evening, look at it carefully—you'll see that it seems more welcoming to you than the others surrounding it. Isn't the warmth and acceptance waiting there for you as real as the warmth of a fire? That is what family can mean to you.

But sometimes you really don't want to be "smothered" by love. You rebel against your family's "interference" with your life. When your new sense of independence, you angrily thrust them away and reject what is offered or demanded of you.

Home is not just where you live but where they understand you.

But even your parents' strictness is an example of their love. It has been said that,

"No" can mean that parents care!

I remember one time when I was about sixteen years old, feeling the force of family rules and being grateful for it.

Everyone attended the Friday-night dances in our town. Even the airmen from the nearby base were welcome to enjoy the chance to socialize and meet new friends. But my family had a very strict rule. "You *never* accepted a ride home unless you already knew the young man."

One night, in a reckless and perhaps rebellious mood, I went against this rule and found myself alone in a car with a boy I had just met, a sophisticated serviceman from the base. I certainly didn't know him. In fact, I had only shared two dances with him. And he wasn't taking me home!!

I talked and talked, insisting that I wasn't "that kind of girl," but it didn't seem to make any difference. We kept traveling off into the dark night, and soon I wasn't sure exactly where we were. I really don't know just what he had in mind for me—but I knew one thing for certain: I had gotten myself into a situation that I couldn't handle.

Fortunately I had been taught that if you thought out events before you got yourself involved, you would know what to do. I knew that the one thing I had to do was to get myself out of that car!!

Although we were miles from home, there were no houses anywhere around, and I was scared to death, I mustered my courage, got out of the car, and started walking off into the dark.

I finally got home about three hours late. All the lights were on in the house and I knew that I was in trouble!

But I was so grateful for my father's anger. It showed his concern and love. I knew that I had been wrong and was so relieved to be home safely. I welcomed the punishment given to me.

Since then, I have learned from personal experience that the longest minutes in a parent's life come when you are lying awake in the dark hours of the night, waiting for an overdue teenager to return home. I am grateful for curfew rules that are usually carefully honored.

No One Cares What I Do

Sometimes the problem might not be an overly-strict parent—it might be just the opposite. The busy tempo of today's world is taking its toll on families. There's not always time left to go around to everyone. If your parents seem to lack interest in the details of your life, it could be that they have a real lack of time or energy left over from their own difficulties and responsibilities. Your mother probably has pressures on her that you can't even imagine. When you add to them, with your own problems, she might just lack the ability to cope with it all.

If you are aware when there are pressures on her, you can help out at those times. Test the temperature of her "busy-ness" mood and proceed with caution. Your mother *wants* to have time to help you. She *is* willing to talk over your problems. If you are considerate in your demands, she will be far more able to help you and talk with you. A good time for a long talk would be when you share *her* work as you talk. Many problems have been solved doing dishes, peeling carrots, canning peaches, or washing windows together.

Your time of life has often been called the "terrible teens." Studies have been made that show that it takes just about the same amount of parental time and energy to raise a child through his teen years as it does to take care of a tiny dependant baby. Admittedly, most of the parent's effort with a baby is physical—washing, changing, feeding, caring for her when she is sick, staying up nights when she is fussy. But the nervous energy required of parents to keep up with the activities now—for them to be *where* you need them to be *when* you need them there—plus the physical care of feeding, clothing, cleaning up afterwards, and staying up nights waiting for you—is just as much of a strain. No wonder the hair of parents begins to grey about the time they have teenagers. A father remarked,

Teenagers are also parent-agers.

I have often likened my job as the parent of a teenager to the role of a choreographer. My major responsibility these last few years has been to make sure that each *body* is in its assigned place, clothed, fed, and properly prepared, at the right time. Your mother probably feels the same way.

Trouble Seems To Always Be My Fault

Your family is having to learn to adjust to the "new you" that you are becoming. It is often hard, especially if you are the oldest, or the youngest, for your parents to allow you to grow up. They are used to handling you as the child you were and have to adjust to your new personality and abilities. Sometimes your very presence acts like a catalyst. (A catalyst is something that reacts with other elements in a mixture and changes them.) If you have younger children in the family group, you often might tease them so much that your coming into the room can change a peaceful situation into a frantic one.

But you also can be the one to calm the family when they are uptight, because of how you react to a situation. As you grow into a mature young adult, you will become a friend to your parents—someone whose company they enjoy on an adult level. They will welcome your ideas and suggestions.

I Want To Be Alone

"My family is always bugging me! My mother nags at me about cleaning my room; my little brother is always messing around in my stuff, my little sister won't keep away from me, and my dad thinks that I need to be with the family. I wish I could just lock the door on them all. I want privacy!"

You don't feel like being with anyone sometimes. You want to close yourself in your room and not see anyone!! In your desire to grow up, you do have a fierce need for quiet times by yourself. And you should be able to have *some*. But . . .

Too often you use these times to shut yourself off from everyone. You don't have the right to privacy if your presence is needed somewhere or if you have a job to complete. This is just a "cop-out."

And sometimes a person might want to be alone all the time. This is wrong! These people need to have people around them to bring themselves out of their selfish feelings and help them forget their troubles. Always shutting herself off from others will make a person more unhappy and cause her bad feelings to expand. Don't mope around for a lengthy time by yourself. Allow the presence of others to bring you out of your "black moods." The effort you make to be with people when you don't want to be will be worthwhile. You will have the ability to change your own attitude towards yourself because you stopped thinking only about yourself.

You have to get rid of ugly and black feelings or they eat away on the inside of you and create ugly sores on your spirit. One possible way to do this is to write out your feelings with a heavy black felt-tip pen. Get all your anger out where you can see it.

Then, fold up the paper and put it away in a safe place where you can forget it. Or make a little ceremony out of tearing up the paper (or burning it, if permitted) and you will usually find that the anger is destroyed along with the paper.

I'm Ashamed Of My Family

Teenagers have many ideals. They expect the world to be perfect. You want all those around you to be perfect, too. This expectation is impossible for your family to meet because they are just human beings, learning and making mistakes just like you are. But as an idealistic teenager, you sometimes reject the whole person instead of the particular fault he may have. Your family member feels the rejection, and the feelings between you are strained even further.

It is easy for you to see what is wrong in the lives of others. But you usually can't do much to change them. You can try with patience and love to show them the way to live. But you can also live better in an uncomfortable situation if you can adopt the proper attitude about it.

Remember the story of the young girl who was ashamed of her home and her inactive parents? She spent all her spare time with a good friend, ignoring her own family. The friend's family were all active in the church—the father was a faithful priesthood holder, the mother a loving homemaker. As the girl returned home on Christmas eve from a special family night with her friend, she shut herself away from her family and cried. Her dingy surroundings, her half-drunk father, and bitter mother were more than she could stand. She tried to savor the thought of what Christmas was like at her friend's, and longed for change in her family. The next morning she was surprised to find one package under the tree for her. In it was a beautiful, expensive dress that her father had sacrificed to buy for her. She realized the depth of her father's love for her as they wept together. Her situation didn't change that Christmas morning; but her days were made a little easier as she built a better attitude towards her parents based on that love.

Learn to respect what *is* good in your family and expect good *from* them. Just as the "as if" principle works when you try to change yourself, it will work in your attitude towards others. Treat them as if they were treating you the way you want them to. They will begin to treat you in that way. It's a twist on the "golden rule." As you expect good things from them, your heart will open up and you will be more able to accept what they are now. The permanent situation might not even change but you can be more comfortable in it, and still keep yourself growing towards what you want to become. Remember,

I am only one, but still I am one.
I cannot do everything, but still I can do something.

I'm Building For My Future Family

If your home life isn't all that you want it to be now, there is another important aspect to remember. You are now preparing for the family you will have in the future. You are becoming a young woman with talents and abilities. You will attract a certain type of young man to you. His talents and abilities, coupled with yours, will determine what kind of family you will build together. Your children will be blessed, or hampered, by what you develop into right now.

You can make plans and resolutions now about what kind of family you want to have and carry them out in later years. You have the power to create a perfect family life for your own children.

And you are also developing what relationships you will have with your family when you are all adults. If you work towards a closeness to your brothers and sisters now, they could be your best friends when you all grow up. You'll want to share your life with them and will enjoy being together.

Even little brothers grow up and have families. If you only think of your brother as a mean tease, not worthy of your time, the two of you will have a harder time being friends as adults. As you build your friendships now, your life together twenty years from now will be more pleasant.

You are fortunate if you have little brothers and sisters (or nieces and nephews) in your home. Spend some of your precious time with them. Don't begrudge your babysitting chores. Little children can help you be less selfish if you open up to them.

One of my sons went through a very stormy thirteenth year, in which he often was very impatient and resentful of his family. But he had a very special two-year-old sister. She would always seek him out, asking for a hug or a kiss. Even in his most rebellious moments, he couldn't resist her love. He found it hard to remain angry with the rest of the family with her around too. A special bond grew between them that still exists today.

The little ones in your home will also help you learn the skills of good mothering, too. You won't be afraid to diaper or bathe your own first baby if you have helped with such chores for others. You can practice being the kind of mother you want to be on them.

My Family Is Forever

This motto is really true. The major reason for going through life is to prepare yourself to be worthy to live together in a family situation throughout eternity. Godhood is parenthood, and the highest level of the Celestial Kingdom will be a place where Gods, who are parents, live surrounded by their offspring. The purpose of Godhood is to create and people other earths with your own spirit children.

The poet Robert Frost has said,

> **Home is the place where once you have to go there they have to take you in.**

Another poet explained,

> **All you'll get from strangers is surface pleasantry or indifference. Only someone who loves you will criticize and help you.**

Your family is your strength. They are your personal cheering section and your source of happiness. Your greatest joys and your deepest sorrows can be shared with them. Love them and you can be blessed with them throughout eternity.

A Friend Is Someone Who Likes You

Linda lived in a ward with a very large Mia Maid class. But somehow she didn't seem to fit into any of the several smaller groups that existed in the class. Sometimes Tina and Ruth would sit by her at Mutual, but usually they would plunk down on the other end of the row and keep on talking to each other. Sally would talk to her at church, but if they passed each other at school, she wouldn't speak. Candy and Pam were just rude—they would make remarks about her, loud enough for Linda to hear. She tried to ignore them both.

Their advisor worked to draw the group together, but it was so split up that they didn't seem to want to like each other. In her discouragement, she finally decided to just worry about giving a good lesson each week.

In an effort to give Linda an opportunity to grow, her advisor asked her to serve on a youth conference committee. But Linda felt uncomfortable in that group also and didn't attend meetings regularly. She ended up doing a poor job with the assignment. This caused her to become even more withdrawn from her class. Soon, it was hard to remember if Linda had been in class or not.

One day, a new adult leader referred to Linda as being inactive. The class presidency was startled. Most of them hadn't even thought of Linda in a long time and they discussed the problem. "She was from an active family—why wasn't she coming out to church?"

Sandy reported that she had noticed Linda talking in the hallway at school with a girl who had a very questionable reputation. As they talked, everyone began to realize that Linda had cut all her ties with the ward and neighborhood girls.

This true story of Linda (only names were changed) doesn't have a happy ending. She drifted further into her friendship with those of questionable reputation and adopted their standards and way of life. She is now unhappily married and completely inactive in the church.

Do you feel like Linda sometimes? Do you go to school, spend the day there and come home without a single person your age speaking to you? You watch the others in groups—laughing and joking, and wish that someone would like you. Feeling wanted and being accepted by others is probably the most tramautic problem that a girl your age can face right now.

Ins and Outs

Young teenage girls are very inclined to form themselves into cliques. These are groups of girls so close together as friends that they can't be friendly (or sometimes even nice) to anyone else. The sad thing about a clique is that deep hurts can be caused to those who are excluded from it. Lifetime problems of low self-esteem can occur.

Another problem about a clique is that they sometimes change and some find themselves left out of their group of friends some day. This creates what we could call the "Ins" and the "Outs."

An "In" is a person who feels comfortable in the group. She feels like her ideas are acceptable and she interacts with the others well. The "Out" is a girl that either is not accepted by the group at all or she is on the outer edges socially. She feels out of place and seldom participates with the others. She will not come to social events on her own and when she is brought by others, she feels uncomfortable there.

The position of being an "In" or an "Out" might change very rapidly. It might even change from group to group. For instance, you might feel accepted by your group at church but you might feel very uncomfortable at school—even sometimes with the very same girls. Your social groups will change depending upon where you are.

Outside things can change the groups, too. A new girl might move in and this would cause the whole clique-system to change. Time passing and the girls maturing and seeking new interests will also change friendship patterns.

Each of you have felt like you were ''In'' and accepted, or ''Out'' and uncomfortable, many times. You know what it can feel like to be lonesome in a group of people. Don't close up friendships so tightly that no one else can feel accepted around you. It is possible to have groups of good friends without meanly excluding others.

Nobody Accepts Me

You might have felt this way for years. You are lonesome to be included as part of a group. Feeling like an ''Out'' can last for a very long time. What can you do about that *now*?

These challenges aren't always sad either. A person who is often alone can go a long way in developing her own personality and her own creativity. She doesn't have to rely on others for companionship and interests. If she is able to accept her alone state, she can become a good student, musically proficient, or excel in other areas. But if she can't be comfortable being alone, then she should try to change herself. Remember Jennie and her personality changes.

Remember, though, that when you are well accepted by your circle of friends you tend to go along with the crowd. You might be afraid to speak out on a subject or to do anything that is too different. You should be sure that you want to pay that price for being accepted.

Friendship is so important to most of you now, though, that you'll seek it wherever you can find it. If you can't feel comfortable with or find acceptance in the natural groups (neighborhoods, church age groups, school classmates), you will look elsewhere.

The ''parking-lot crowd'' will be very accepting at first to a lost ''Out'' looking for friends. But theirs is a very limiting type of friendship. It is based upon the attitude that ''you act as we act and we will accept you—come down to our level and you can be our friend.'' The girl descends down to their level and the mud and quicksand pulls her right in.

If you are in a leadership position in church or school, be sure you are aware of those girls who are seeking now for friendship. You have an obligation to break down clique barriers. You don't have to completely abolish the groups of girls—you need them to exist—just open them up so they aren't so self-centered that no one else can be accepted by the group. Be kind to an "Out." It might not be too long before the alignment of the group changes and you find yourself on the edges of a group, seeking for friends. If you all could work together as friends, the positions of "Ins" and "Outs" wouldn't be so defined and everyone could be happier together.

It Takes Time to be a Friend

Young girls seem to be naturally selfish. They are interested in themselves. It takes time to be a good friend, and time is one thing that you have very little to spare. You want friends for yourself but don't want to expend the time and effort to be a friend to others.

Sherry moped around. She had no friends. She hated school and didn't ever go to school functions. She didn't like her Mutual or Church classes either because no one ever spoke to her there. She was unhappy at home and often fought with her family. The only pleasure she found in life was eating in front of the television. Naturally, Sherry was getting fatter. In fact, she was fat!

Sherry blamed all her troubles on others.

"If someone would be my friend . . ."
"If Dot would talk to me at school . . ."
"If Betty would invite me to her party . . ."

Sherry didn't think about what *she* had to do to become a friend. She didn't even think that she had to do anything. She never even acted like she wanted anyone to be her friend.

Sherry didn't know—or didn't want to find out—that,

If you want to be liked—
you first have to make yourself likeable.

A girl has to put herself out to be a friend. She has to be in a place where others are, like school functions or church activities. Sitting home and feeling sorry for herself isn't going to change her into anything more than sadder or lonelier.

If you feel friendless like Sherry right now, you can do something about it if you want to. Choose what you want to be different in your life and set your goals. You might want to work on becoming likeable and friendly like Jennie. Perhaps you'd rather concentrate your efforts on developing a talent. Friendships have been made there, too.

Be patient with yourself and your age group. It won't be easy to change yourself, or their friendship, in a few days—or even months. Hopefully your story will have a better ending than Linda's—the girl who stopped trying to be a friend. Her share of the blame was that she gave up trying too soon. It is easy to blame others for your troubles. The hard thing is to do something about your problems yourself.

Friends often go along on the comfortable level of attending the social or church activity but doing as little as possible. It's hard to overcome "we'll do it the easiest way." Somehow the natural laziness of the group comes forth when you try to figure out just how much you should be doing. But if a member will suggest a desire to do more, often the group will follow along willingly. You can raise the standards of your group yourself.

I'm Afraid to Say Anything

Carol had been invited to go to a movie with her friends. Her mother had actually given her permission to go with them! Carol often wondered about the strictness of her parents.

"Surely all movies weren't that bad. And this one had won the Academy Award and other honors. It had to be great!"

About halfway into the movie though, Carol began to feel very uncomfortable. The language of the leading lady was so bad that it embarrassed her to hear a woman talk like that. And there were scenes that showed much more skin than Carol knew was acceptable to what she had been taught. The whole movie was beginning to bother her. Finally she got up quietly, excused herself and went into the lobby. She sat on the bench waiting for the movie to end. One by one her friends came out and joined her. Carol's stand against an improper film had helped them all to live up to what they all knew was right. They went out to eat and spent the rest of the evening talking about better ways to have fun in the future.

Did You Hear About . . .?

Gossip can seem like so much fun. It is interesting to hear about people who live on the edges of right and wrong and how they get away with it. Soon each person adds their own version or bits of the story as they pass on new facts. No one seems to worry if what she is saying might not be true.

Sometimes a girl may even say cruel or untrue things in order to seek the attention or approval of the crowd. Often she would be shocked if she could stand outside of herself and hear herself talking.

The Hawaiians have a good saying:

**A person who talks about his inferiors—
hasn't any.**

Talking about others and gossiping is a two-edged sword. It can cut you down as you cut down others. It has been said that,

To belittle is to be little.

When talking about anyone else, remember the golden rule and say only what you'd like to have said about you.

Remember the story about Bambi? When he was first learning to walk he was very awkward and fell down often. The other little animals laughed with glee at his clumsiness. When Thumper, the little rabbit, said "He doesn't walk so good, does he?", his mother reminded him of his father's rule:

**If you can't say sumpthin' nice 'bout someun,
Don't say nuttin' at all!**

Remember Thumper's advice the next time you have a temptation to pass on a juicy story about someone. You'll be a better friend.

Amy and I Are Best Friends!

If you have a best friend now, you are very fortunate. You can relax and know that someone likes you. Because a best friend is so close to you, she can be very honest with you and yet you aren't offended by her frankness. You trust her, and you know she has your best interests at heart. She should be treasured by you.

Be happy together, but don't hold onto each other so tightly that you exclude others from your circle of friendships. As you grow, your interests usually change. Your best friend of today might not even be a close acquaintance in a year or two, and others may take her place in your life.

Friends are so important to you right now. You need to be a friend to others to help you become less self-centered and more giving. In the story of The Three Musketeers, one of them says a line with a real message for you:

Friendship consists in forgetting what one gives, and remembering what one receives.

Friendship isn't always simple. It isn't something you can have without giving of yourself, too. A very wise woman explained,

Every now and again you meet some radiant, attractive person and you are delighted to find out that they adore you. Then you realize that they adore just about everybody. That's what has made them so radiantly attractive.

You can enrich your life now with friendship by being a good friend. As you do, you prepare for the best friend you will have in this life—that young man who will accept all that you are now and will grow with you eternally.

He's A Boy!!!

"Snips and snails and puppy dog tails . . ." Often you can see these in a seventh-grade boy. Of course by this time, you have grown out of all that Junior High stuff and are ready for a more mature relationship with men. But they are still running around, interested in frogs, kites, snakes, sports, hunting, cars and scouts.

Bobby and Jim were walking home from school one afternoon.

"Do ya think your science fair project will win?" asked Bobby.

"I dunno," answered Jim. "That Sally Smith sure is smart. Her's is good. She'll probably beat us all. Why does she act so smarty?"

"She really does," Bobby replied, "but she's sure silly about boys. Didja see her looking all gooey-eyed at Stan the other day? Probably just because he won the track meet. Girls sure are dumb!"

"Yeah," Jim agreed. "Hey—did ya get your new model of the space ship yet?"

Junior-high-school boys are still little boys in many ways. All your life so far you have been physically, mentally, and even emotionally older than the boys your age. You have been taller, better readers, usually smarter, and often stronger than the boys. Early teenage years are when the boys begin to catch up to you and pass you in development.

Me—Be Friends with a Boy?

Remember when you were young, you probably played a lot with a boy—perhaps were even best friends?

Then the friendship was broken up. A girl was not worth much—she was something to hate, or perhaps useful for chasing around the grade-school playground. Now you are becoming tolerated and useful for teasing again. These years are now the beginnings of social awakening for boys.

They go through this teasing and growing-up stage before they are ready to accept you as a friend again. It's a problem—

you are ready for friendship with them, but they are still running about being obnoxious! You will need a little patience waiting for them to grow up—but they will. In the next four or five years, they will gain all the social graces and maturity you desire. Give them time!!

Don't act superior around the younger-acting boys either. That friend of yours who is barely human in the eighth grade might just grow into the most handsome boy in school by the eleventh grade—or he might have a neat friend—or he might have a brother—or he might even someday become your Stake President!!

So work to establish a friendship with boys again. They are realizing that "girls aren't so bad after all" and soon will begin to enjoy you, too.

I Like Boys Now

Since many, if not most, boys take until they are sixteen or so before they are interested enough in girls to date, you have plenty of time to relax and enjoy them now. You need the time for friendshipping for a few years anyway.

You are fortunate if you have a built-in relationship with a boy right now—a brother, a cousin, or a close neighbor with whom you have been able to talk through the past years.

Boys and girls need to learn how to talk and interact with each other before they reach dating age. If they each haven't learned to carry on interesting conversations and spend their time doing something more than teasing, the dating relationship will suffer. When dating partners can't talk together and become good friends, they will be insensitive and selfish with each other. This can cause arguments, hurt feelings, and many unhappy dating experiences.

So now can be the years of practicing how to talk with boys. They can become friends—not boyfriends, but friends who are boys. You enjoy a boy as a real person, without worrying about if he is looking you over as possible dating material. If you can forget about that magic age of sixteen and just become an interesting person to be around, you'll be happier together.

And be sure that you girls don't talk too much *about* the boys. It's fun to share your excitements of "Guess who talked to me?" with your friends, but a boy's ego can be hurt if you talk too much about his attempts to show his interest in you.

Junior high is when you write a love letter to a
girl you're crazy about—
And she passes it around!

What About Boy/Girl Groups

The groups that form as you become friends with boys will be fun. You practice on how to act with a boy, go places together or have parties. These are your first "group dating" experiences.

One of my sons developed a close group of friends in junior high school. They all enjoyed music and went to concerts together. They often walked home from school together and the girls sometimes would come up with a reason for an impromptu party. They all had fun learning to talk with each other. As the years passed and they turned sixteen, they occasionally dated each other. But the group continued on, mainly as just good friends. Even now as they are marrying (and no one yet has married another one of this group), their friendships continue, and perhaps will for many more years.

So encourage such groups if one seems to be developing among your friends. You can all gain from such an experience.

Boys Have Pressures Too

The same type of physical and emotional changes that you are feeling now are felt by the boys, too. They are growing up in the same ways that you are. But it seems that they have to choose right or wrong actions sooner than girls do. For whatever the reason—whether society expects them to grow up faster, or their friends pressure them—by the time a boy is a Teacher in the Aaronic Priesthood, he usually has made some basic decisions about his activity in the church and his spirituality. He seems to drop out of church functions almost altogether for a time, or he remains active in the group.

Boys seem to have to grow up in other matters also. Their social calendar is slower, but the pressure for them to grow up and "act like a man" is there, even if they aren't ready for it. They are fighting to grow up to their own expectations of themselves and other opinions.

Perhaps they would just as soon retreat into the little boy-world of toys and fun.

I'm Ready to Date Now

Many girls are ready to date before they are sixteen. They are interested in older boys and often the temptation to accept the early dating patterns can be too much for them. But there are many good reasons for the age of sixteen to be declared as the appropriate time to begin dating, such as,

1. You really aren't ready, even if you think that you are. You haven't lived the years to have time to grow up yet. There are still many fun experiences and exciting opportunities to enjoy before you enter the frustrations of dating.
2. You cheat yourself of experiences when you try to skip a life stage. You need the preparation of the pre-dating boy/girl relationship in your life. When you skip this and begin to date in junior high school, something will be missing from your growth pattern and you'll have to mature in that way later on.
3. Life is now. You don't have to wait for living to begin. You probably have heard the observation older folks make that "Life is too short to be wasted upon the young." Perhaps you have even resented an older person telling you that you were trying to grow up too fast. When you are impatient to find out if life will be better "when I can date," "when I graduate," "when I go to college," or "when I get married," you miss part of living. You don't have to wait until when—. Enjoy what you are doing now.
4. You push your experiences too early. If dating has begun at too early an age, you soon run out of things to do. A movie and something to eat afterwards can get pretty boring night after night. It often follows that you experiment with newer sensations before you are ready and able to handle them. Trouble begins for everyone. I don't just mean the obvious sexual temptations either. I've seen many steady couples break up because they became bored to death with each other. They had "done it all." Teenage life is a time for fun. Adults look

back upon their teens with longing at all the crazy things they did. Keep the excitement in your teen years by not growing up into a dating relationship too soon.

5. Most boys your age aren't ready for dating yet. When you date older boys, you miss out on lots of the fun things a girl your age should be enjoying.

6. Probably the one reason that should be good enough to stand alone without any other arguments is that President Kimbal has told you not to date until you are sixteen.[1]

Dating Sounds Like Fun!

The telephone rings and a deep voice is on the other end.

"Uh Kathleen, uh—this is Bill. Well—I was wondering if you'd like to go out with me?"

Have you ever wondered what a boy goes through to get to that stage? The simple desire to be with a young lady turns into a major project for him. You worry about "Will he ask me out?" His concerns are,

"Who do I ask?"
"What do I ask her to do?"
"Who do we do it with?"
"How do we get there?"
"Can I afford it?"
"Will she go with me?" etc.

And it can be very expensive. Even an average movie date costs so much now that you really have to be worth it.

The dating game is much more involved than your dreams make it out now. Perhaps that's why so many young men spend

1. For instance, see President Spencer W. Kimball, *Church News*, August 24, 1974, in which he said any dating or pairing off in social contacts should be postponed until at least the age of 16 or older, and even then there should be much judgment used in selections and in seriousness; See also his comments in "The Marriage Decision," *Ensign*, Vol. 5, February, 1975, p. 4.

so much time at the girls home. It's easier to just "drop by for a visit" than to plan the production of a date.

You can get ready for those times by learning some fun and easy snacks to prepare. (Boys will always be hungry!) And you can also learn to get along with your family now. When *he* is dropping by, you don't want to be fighting with your brother in front of him. Perhaps you can get your brother to teach you how to play chess now instead. Then you will have an interesting game to play those cold winter nights in the future.

Just Wait Til I'm 16!

Probably the most unfair social calamity is the girl who waits faithfully until she is old enough to date—and then no one asks her!! It seems to happen frequently and there really isn't too much that a girl can do about it all.

She can ask someone to the girl's-choice affairs and perhaps break the dating ice this way. Sometimes other people try to arrange blind dates or invitations to parties for her. But the important thing to remember is this: try to not be hurt by the unfair blow that life has dealt you. There are probably lots of boys around you who will be grateful for a girl who expects nothing more than friendship. That's not exactly what dreams are made of, but it's better than nothing at all.

Another unfair part of this problem is that the non-dating girls always seem to share a Laurel class with at least one girl who seems to have dozens of boys after her—and she is not even interested in dating and rather bored with the whole idea!! But no one ever promised that everything would come out even in life.

As a young man enters high school, he is forced to become aware of career decisions and preparations for his missionary service. He has to plan out his life, year-by-year, much sooner than you do. You have many decisions to make and skills to learn, too. But remember that life becomes real for boys very early.

Boys are special creatures. You look forward to the day when you will be swept away by your own knight in shining armor. And he'll probably come (although he might not exactly sweep you away, and might have dents in his armor—and perhaps he won't even own a horse!).

But he probably won't even be someone that you know right now. Studies show that if you don't marry while you are still a high school student (and you aren't even considering that early of a marriage, I hope!) you don't know your husband yet. Of the hundreds of young women that I have worked with and known in the last twenty years, less than 5% have married boys they grew up with—or even knew in high school.

So relax and enjoy the boys that you know right now. You will be friends for another few years and then you will all go on to something more. Your future husband is growing up somewhere, surrounded by other girls. He is practicing his social skills with them now and when you meet you will be ready for each other. Be sure you'll be properly prepared for him, too.

I Am A Daughter of God

Do you ever feel homesick when you are home? Have you felt lonesome and alone, even when you were with other people? Do you seem to be seeking for something, but you aren't really sure what?

Part of your growing up challenge will be to try to develop a personal relationship with God. As you find out who you are you will not feel lonesome. Your study of the principles of the gospel will show that you have a Father in Heaven. This eternal being is the Father of your spirit. You were raised in His presence as a spirit child. He loves and cares for you in the same way as your earthly father does.

Your Father in Heaven desires you to return and live near Him forever. When you sing the song about being a "child of God," you are speaking of Him.

He has sent His son, Jesus Christ, to be the God of this world and its Savior. Christ's atonement paid for the sins of the people of the world. When you personally accept this sacrifice as a payment for your own sins, you also accept Jesus as your Savior. He holds His atonement out as a gift for you. You can accept it and be forgiven of your sins as you repent of them. Jesus Christ cares for you and seeks for your happiness, also.

Sometimes you might feel that no one around you understands your problems. When you feel this aloneness, try to find time for quiet reflection and meditation. Go somewhere to be alone and let your mind turn toward the Savior. As you think of what He has done for you and how He cares for you, it can bring comfort and peace of mind to your soul. You will find a certain knowledge of your self-worth in His eyes.

Except You Become Converted

Many of you have been taught the principles of the Gospel from the time you have first been aware. But now it is important for you to find out for *yourself* if everything you were taught is true.

In a sense, every active adult member of the Church is a convert to it. Some have joined because they were taught by the missionaries, changed their life style and were baptized. Others were born into Latter-day Saint families. But there has been a point in their lives when they said "Yes, it is all true. I know that for myself!"

They might not remember exactly when they made the commitment. But often it can be traced back to a specific testimony-building incident. They all have been personally converted to the gospel of Jesus Christ.

When I was fifteen, I struggled with some of the questions that many active LDS youths have about the gospel. But one particular event that year still stands as a basic building block to my testimony.

An LDS Institute chapel had been built on the campus of a nearby University and President David O. McKay was coming to offer the dedicatory prayer. All the seminary students were invited to attend the services.

We had to go very early to get seats. I remember sitting with my friends in the chapel waiting for the meeting to begin. I began to think about President McKay, wondering when I would really know for myself that he was the Prophet of God.

Finally the doors opened at the front of the chapel and a small group of men walked in. In the center was a tall white-haired man dressed in a dark suit. As the audience recognized him as President McKay and rose to its feet as a sign of respect, I suddenly knew, "He is the prophet of God." I could feel the Holy Spirit filling me with that knowledge. It was as real as if I were being flooded with water. I wanted to shout out loud and tell everyone, so certain was I that he was truly God's chosen servant.

That knowledge has stayed with me ever since, and the Holy Ghost has confirmed the same testimony of the succeeding

Presidents of the Church. I can really say that I *know* that our Church is led by Prophets of God.

You are now beginning this striving for your own testimony. As you do so, it will be natural for you to seek and wonder about what you have been taught. The Seminary program and other classes of the Church are excellent places for you to begin your study. It is not wrong to ask questions about the gospel. It shows that you are entering into the seeking and growing process. Trying to learn for yourself is a good and right step for you to take. In fact, it is necessary for you to begin on your own quest for a testimony.

What is wrong is for you to have a question about some particular principle which you leave unresolved. You then allow that question to influence how you feel about the whole gospel. You must not throw away something eternal because of questions. It's like throwing away a valuable ring because you get some bread dough stuck in it.

How Do I Learn to Pray?

Learn to pray by praying. Prayer is much more than just flopping onto your knees on your way to bed. That is what you learned as a two-year-old when you asked for blessings on the dog, the milkman and a whole list of people. And that was fine for you when you were young.

But when you really begin to talk with your God, you will begin to pray. Use proper prayer language, express thankfulness and request blessings. But also take time to ask questions and seek for answers to those questions.

While you are still on your knees, think about the problems you were discussing in your prayer. Open up your mind and let it ask questions about what you were praying. Sometimes, as you do so, you will find that new ideas will flood into your mind. As they expand, you will realize that they are answers that you were seeking. Occasionally the answer will be expressed as a complete thought, or you may even hear a voice speak within you. But often it will just be a growing of your own thoughts into new ideas. These are answers to your prayers.

The time you spend on your knees can be valuable in helping you decide how to live your life. But prayer should be used whenever you feel a need.

Your heart can offer up a prayer without you needing privacy to drop to your knees. You can receive answers for a prayer offered silently in public in the same way as new ideas come to you.

But sometimes you feel that you aren't getting through—that your prayers aren't even making it up to the ceiling! You might then decide that it really isn't worth taking the time to pray because you start to feel that "He doesn't care about me anyway. I'm just an insignificant person. It doesn't matter what I do so I won't bother Him any more. He never answers me."

That is exactly what Satan is wanting you to do. His tools of discouragement and self-pity are a powerful force in your life right now. Satan is a real being—just as the Father and Jesus Christ are. And the Devil desires to have you discouraged and unhappy.

The Championship Game

Life could be said to be like a championship basketball game. You are the star player on one side. The other players on your team are your family, friends, and all the others who care about you. You have God and the angels in heaven, and all those in church leadership positions here on earth in the stands cheering for you.

The opposing team is made up of the evil forces in the world. Their cheering section is filled with Satan and His hosts of devils.

Sometimes you prevail and make a point by overcoming temptations and doing the right thing. When you learn a gospel principle and accept it for yourself, attend a meeting in the face of opposition, or suddenly understand a lesson taught, you can feel as good about it as if you had made a winning basket in front of thousands of people.

Sometimes the opposition prevails and makes the points. When you break a commandment knowingly, cause contention in your family, hurt a person, fail to act when you should, or commit a sin, the cheering for their side can almost be heard out loud. The desolate feelings of failing, at those times, can be overcome by seeking a new game plan and striving to gain the lead again.

God didn't allow you, His precious spirit daughter, to come down to earth without the tools to handle the problems you would have to face. He knew that you had a strong spirit and He knew that you were prepared to withstand temptations. No one promised you that earth life would be easy. In fact, I'm sure that in our pre-mortal life we knew of many of the problems we could encounter. But knowing our strengths and abilities, we probably said something like, "Sure, I can handle that!!" And you can!

The tools to handle our life are developed within the spiritual side of ourselves. As you add the knowledge that Jesus is your Savior, understand the gospel by regular scripture reading and study, and as you attend your meetings and try to gain something from them, your spirit becomes strong. You gain strength to combat the discouraging forces of evil. You are learning how to become perfect in this life.

It is much like a little child learning to walk. She wants to be able to walk and practices walking around furniture for a long time before even trying to get out across the floor. And then, she needs someone to hold out his arms to her and coax her into doing it. She has to try to walk on her own—the other person can't do it for her.

Remember, as a pre-mortal being you knew much of what would happen to you here in your earth life, and you had confidence that you could overcome the challenges. You are on the road to Exaltation now. It can be yours if you aren't afraid to try to reach out for it. Daughter of God, *now* is the time to live.